FOOTBALL

DESIGNER

10

FOR KIDS

COLOURING BOOK

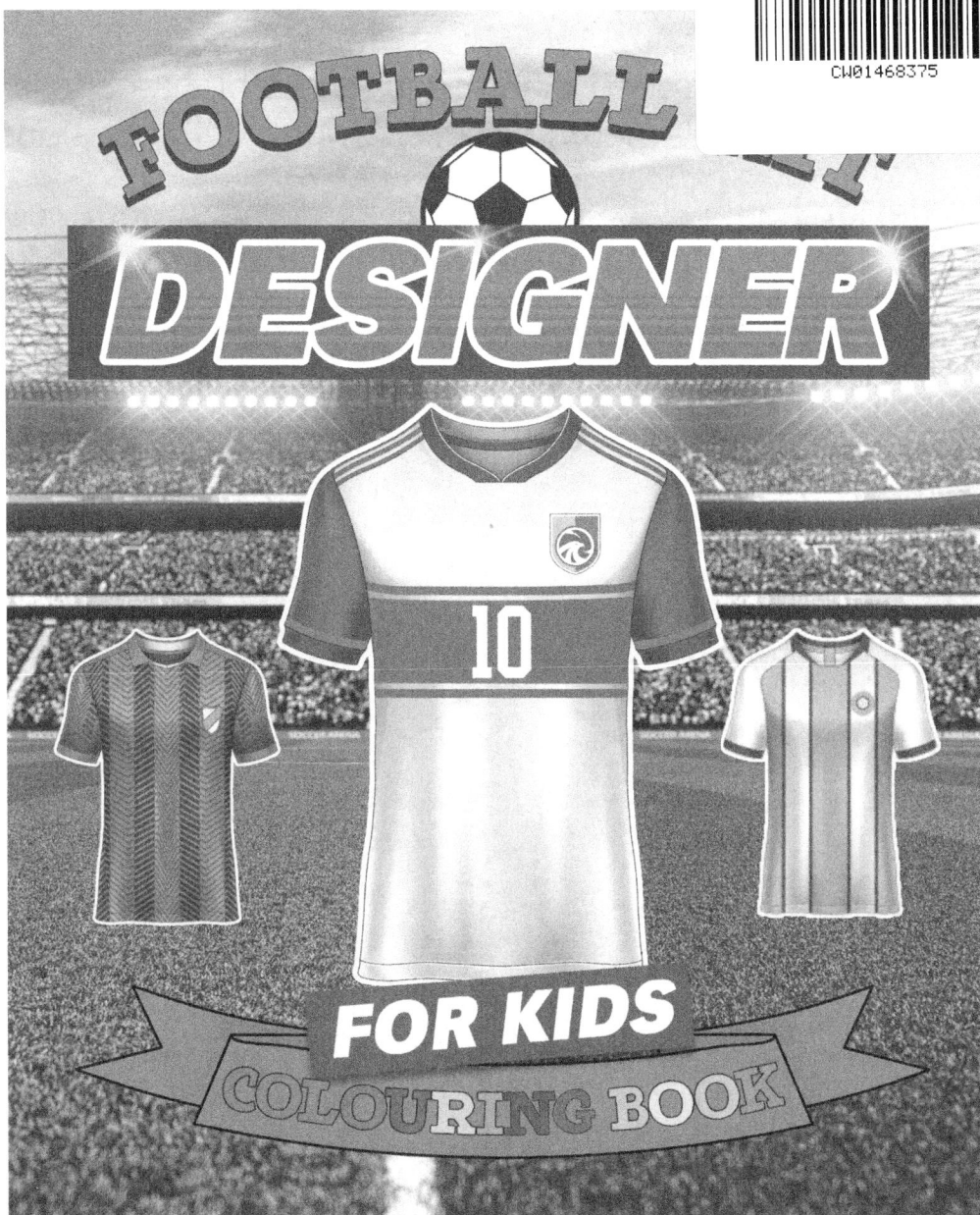

THIS BOOK BELONGS TO

CW01468375

COLOURING IN THE DESIGNS

If using felt tip pens or coloured markers to colour please consider using a sheet of plain paper underneath when colouring in the designs.

Whilst each design has a black coloured rear, some stronger coloured pens can still bleed-through the page, affecting the next design.

Use the blank shield badges to test colour pen / marker bleed-through.

Coloured pencils and crayons should not bleed though the page.

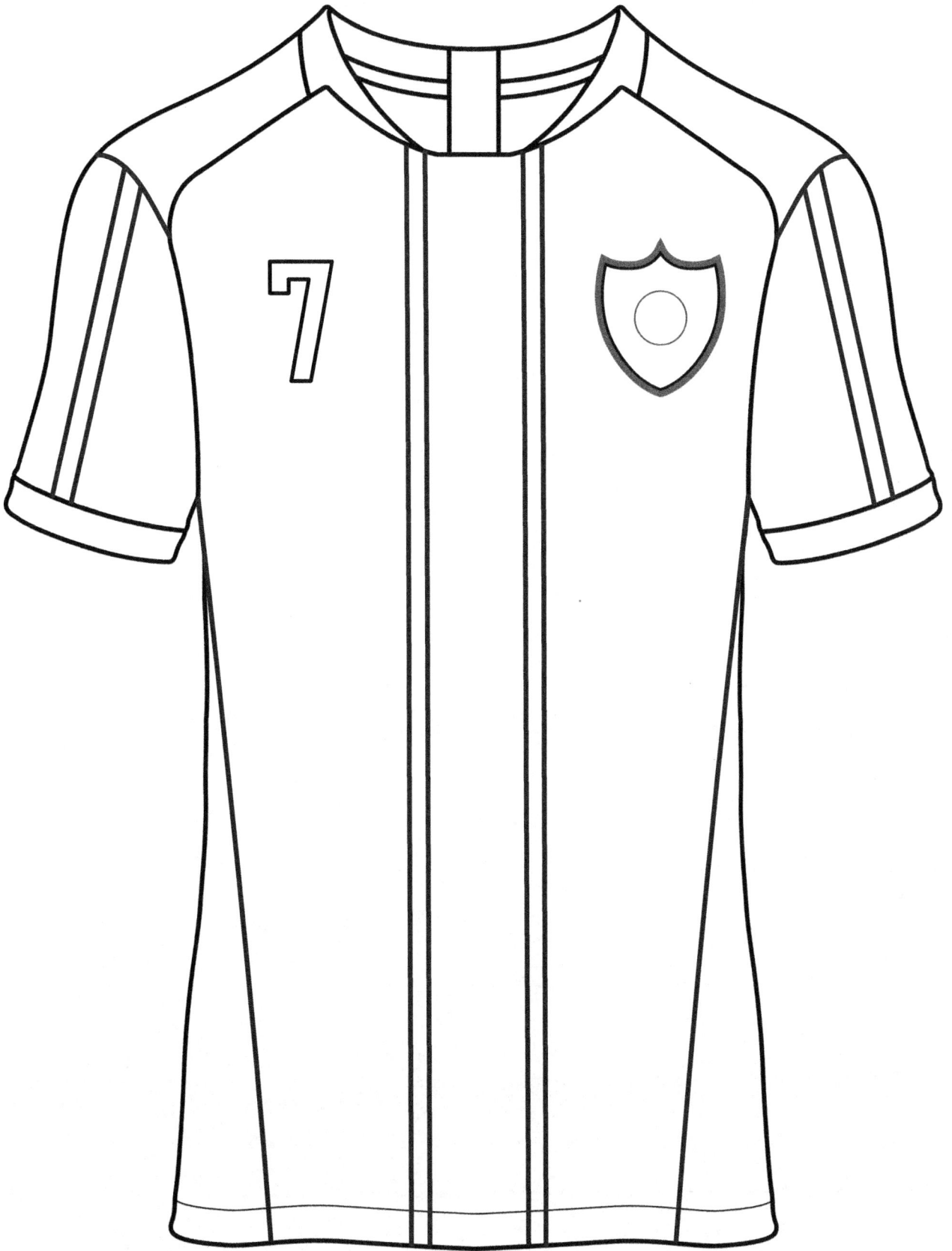

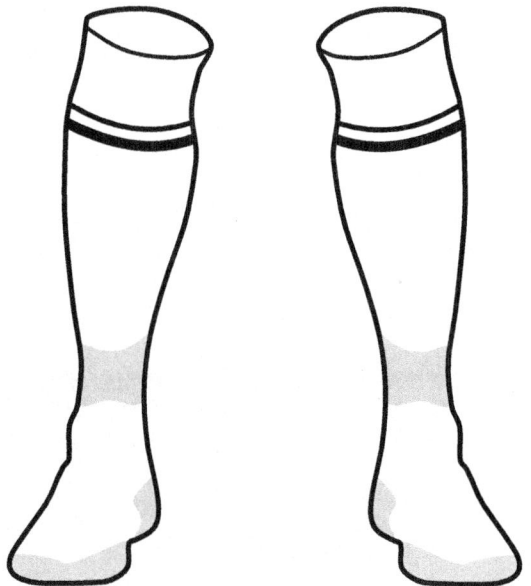

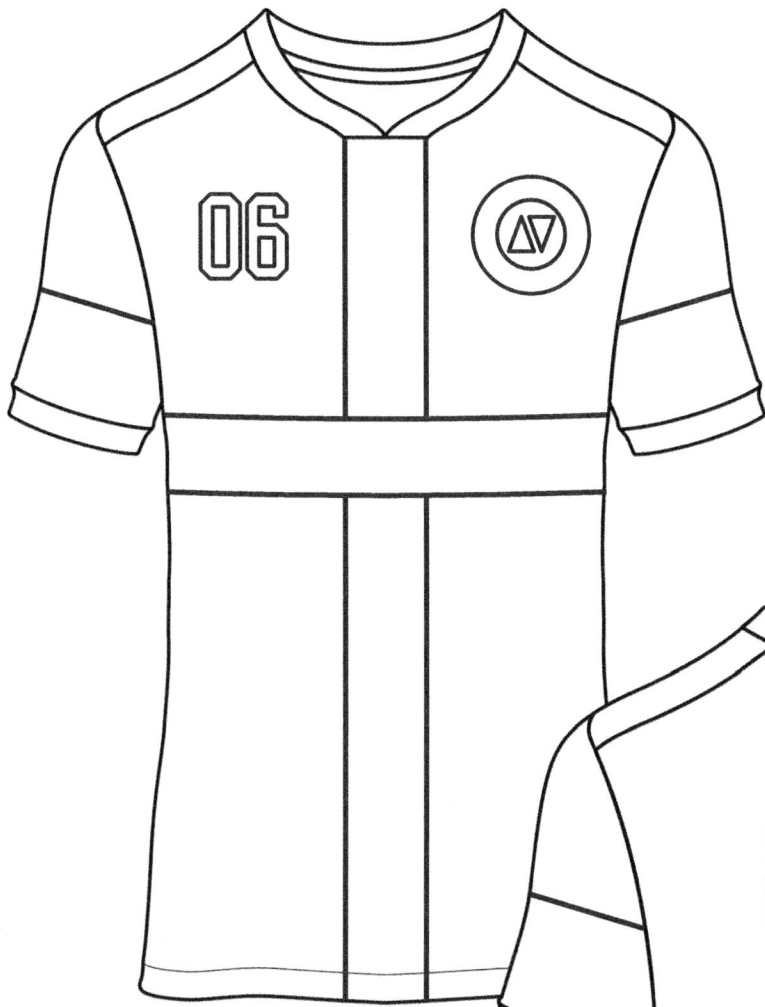

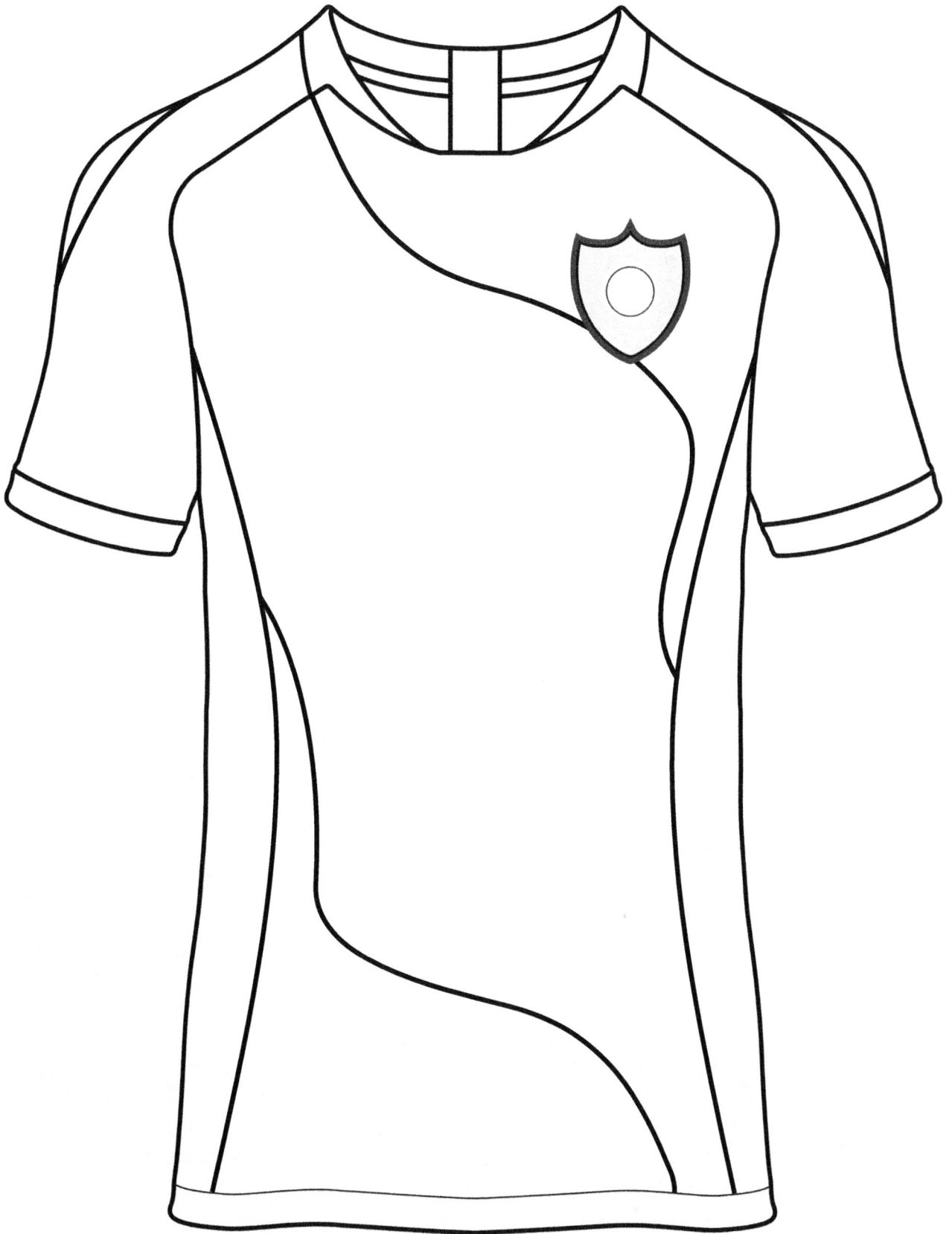

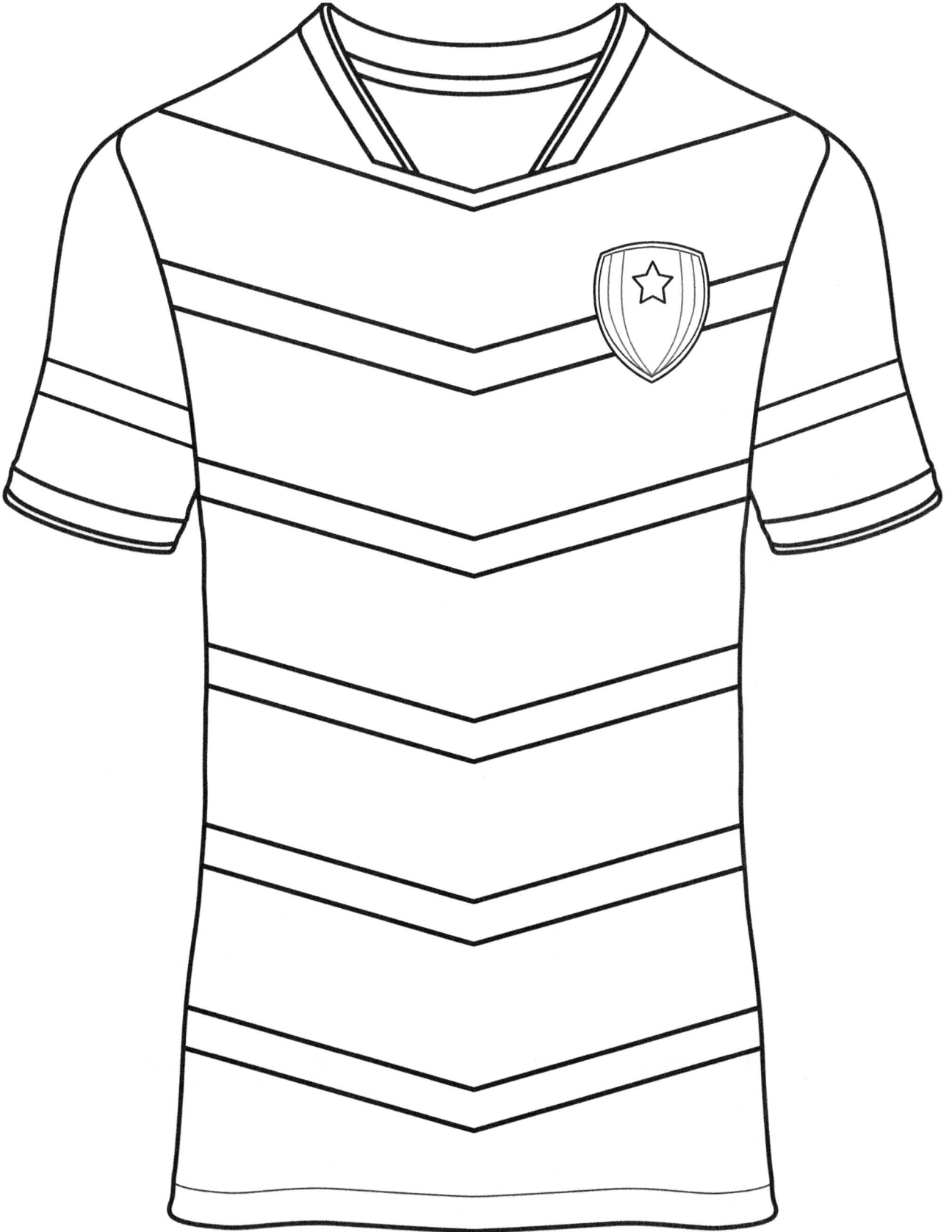

DESIGN YOUR OWN

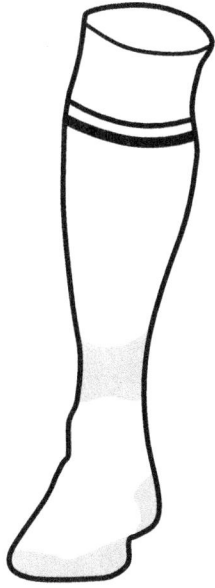

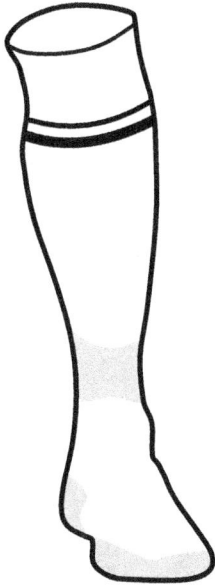

GOALKEEPER'S KIT

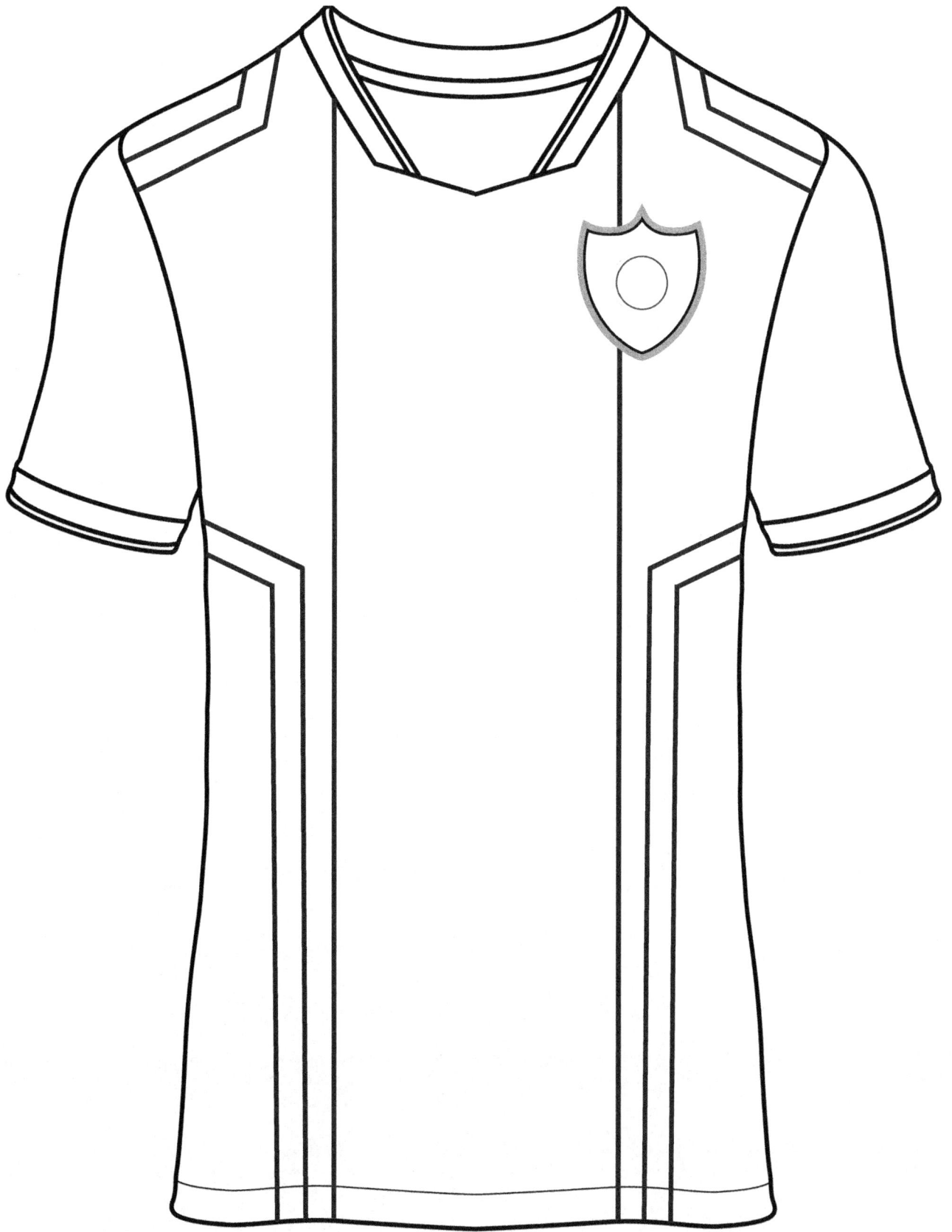

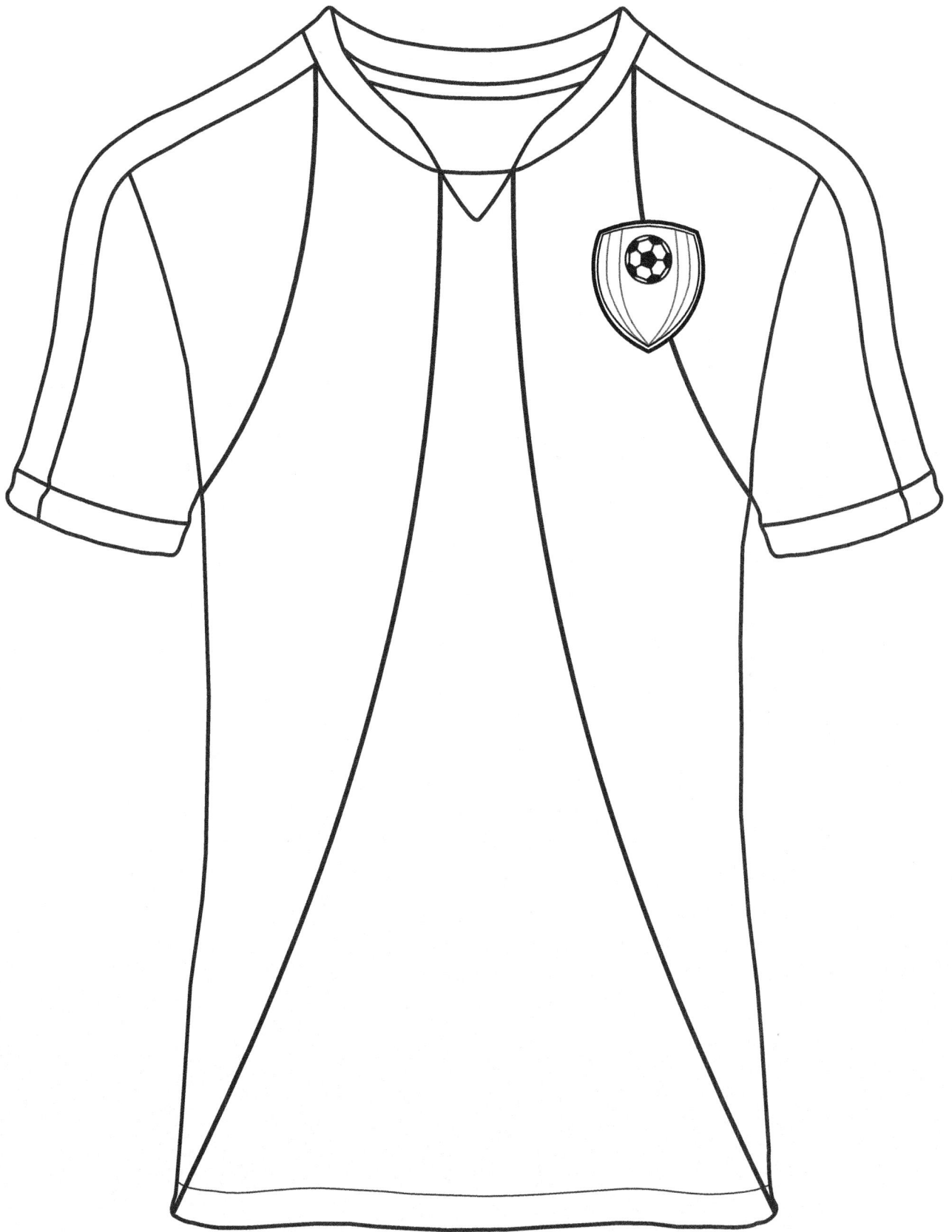

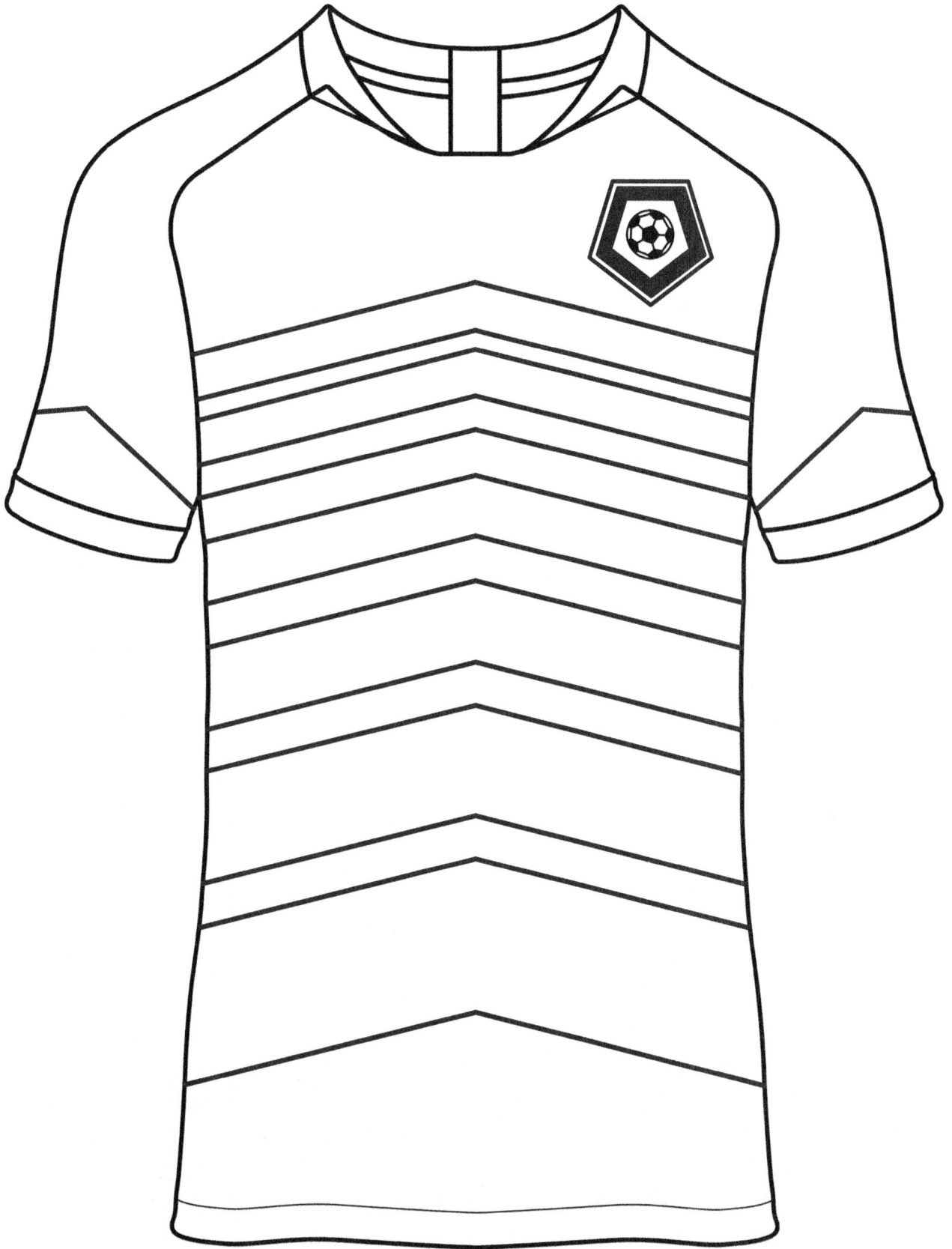

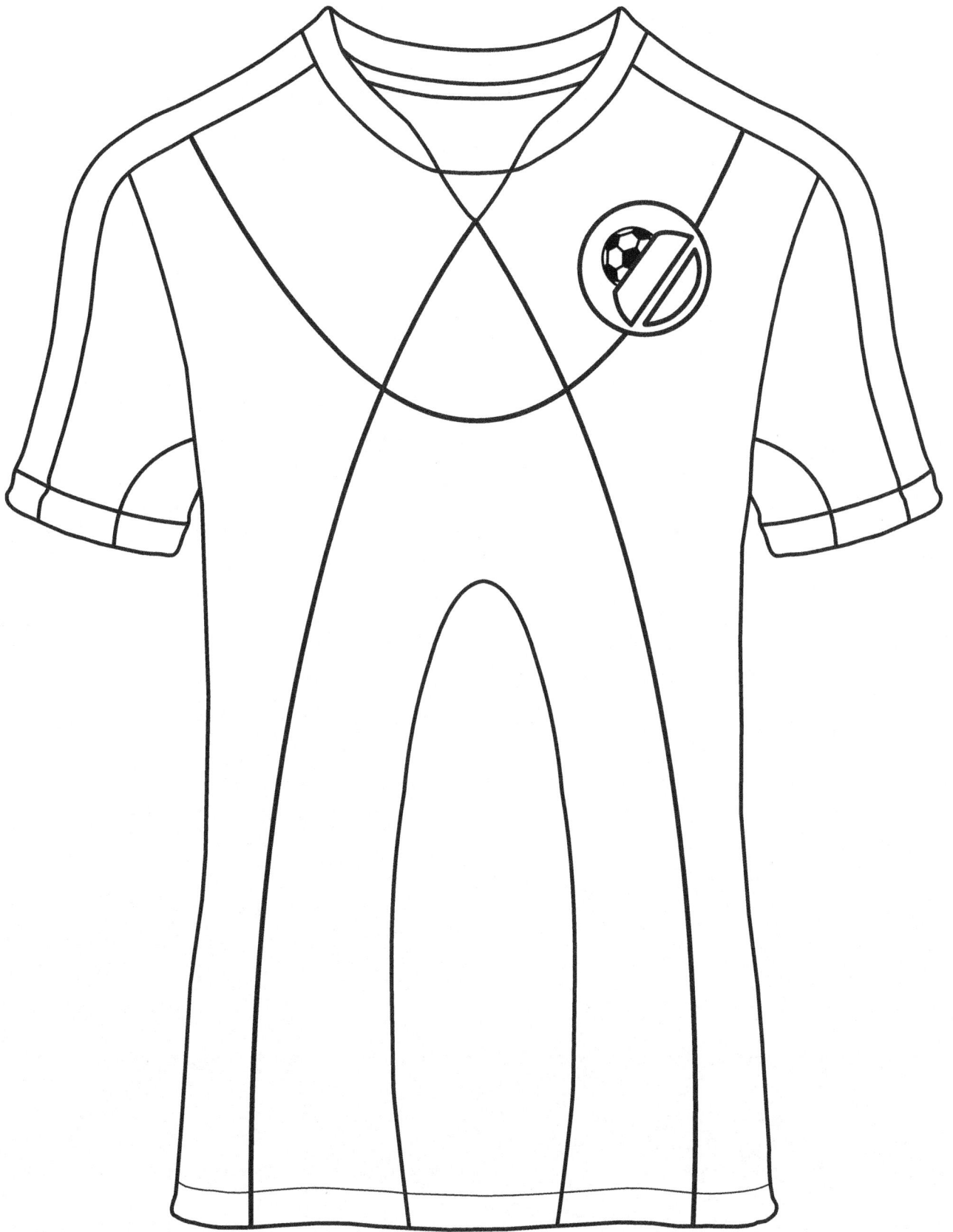

STAR PLAYER

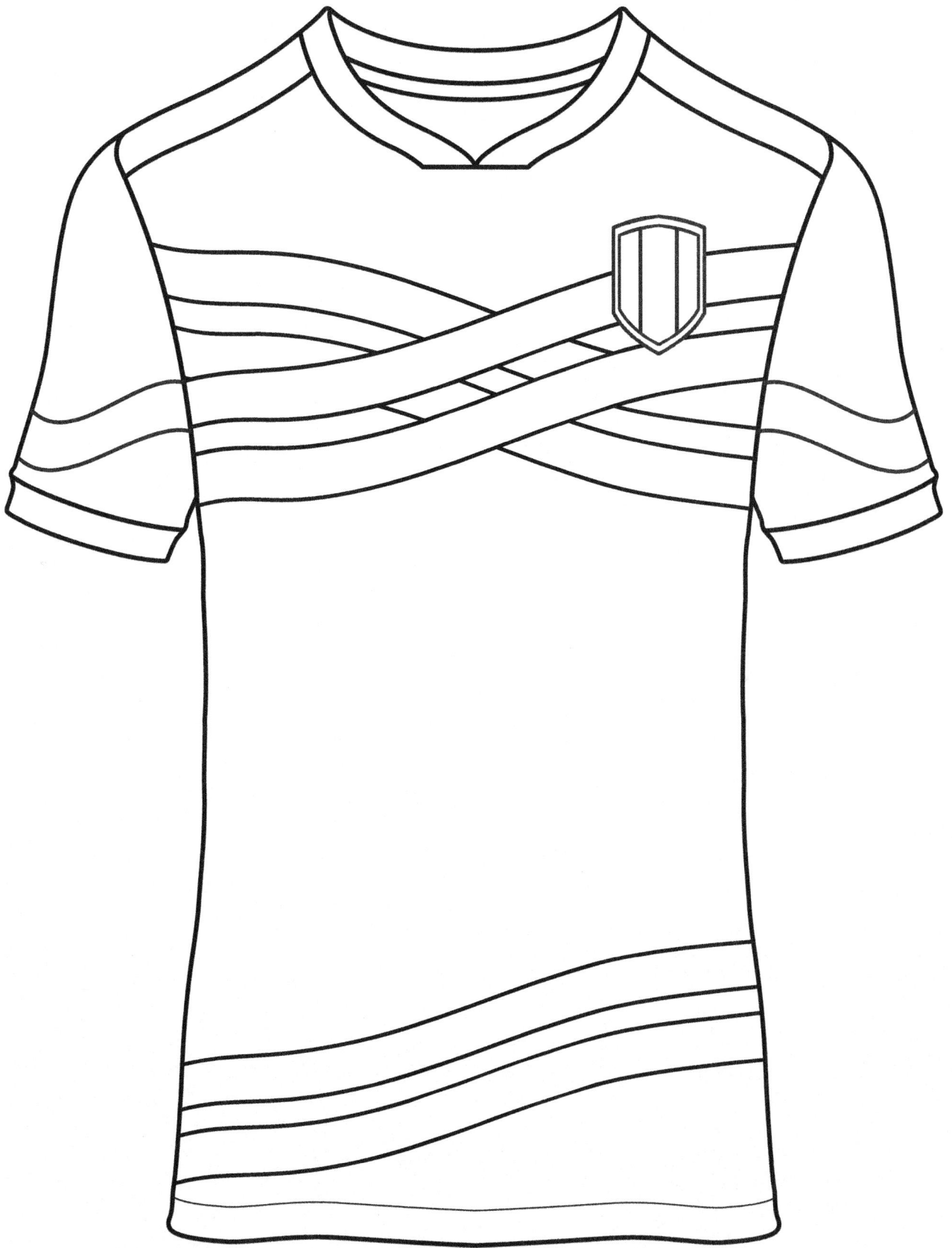

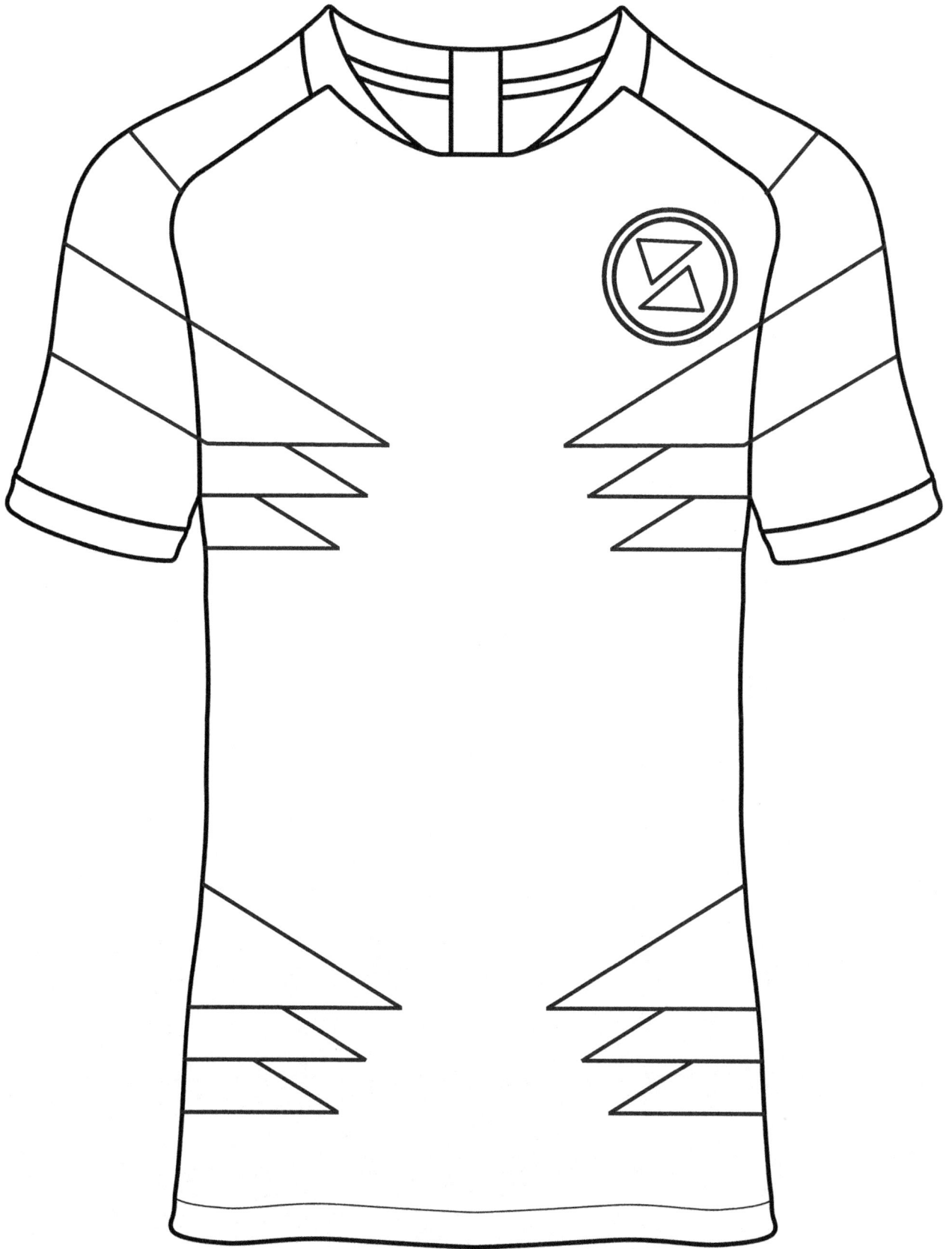

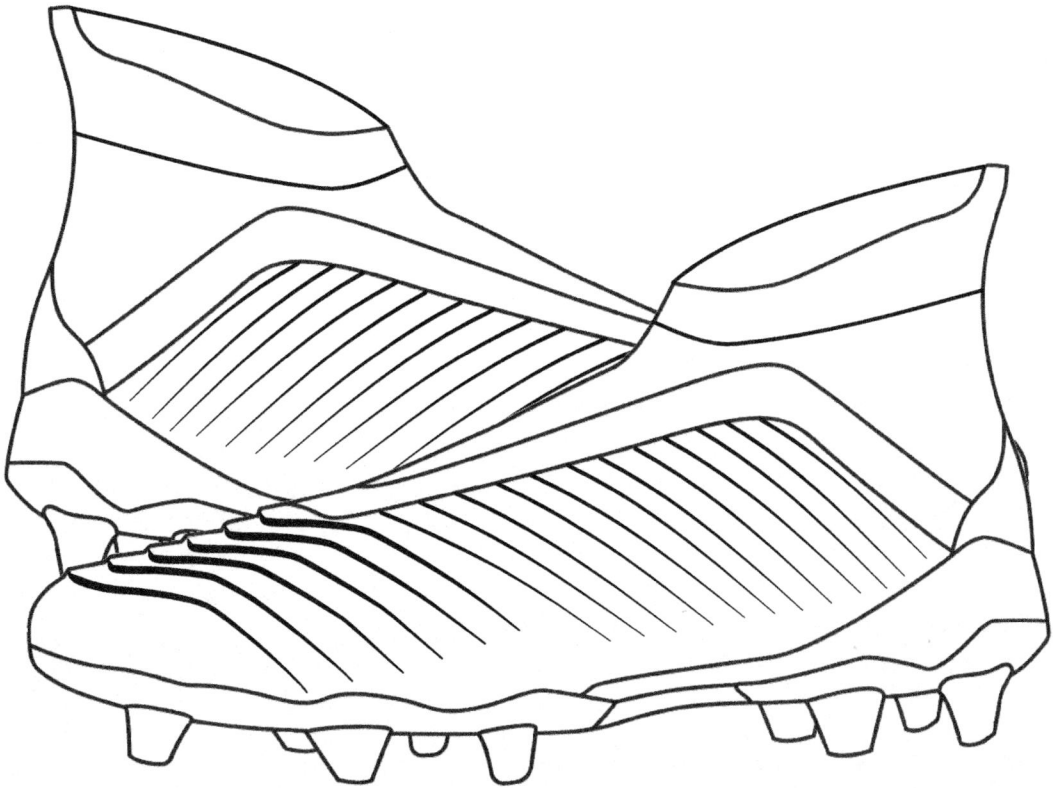

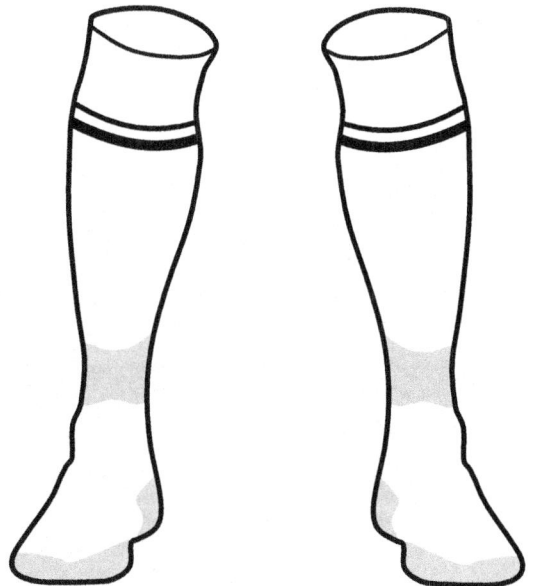

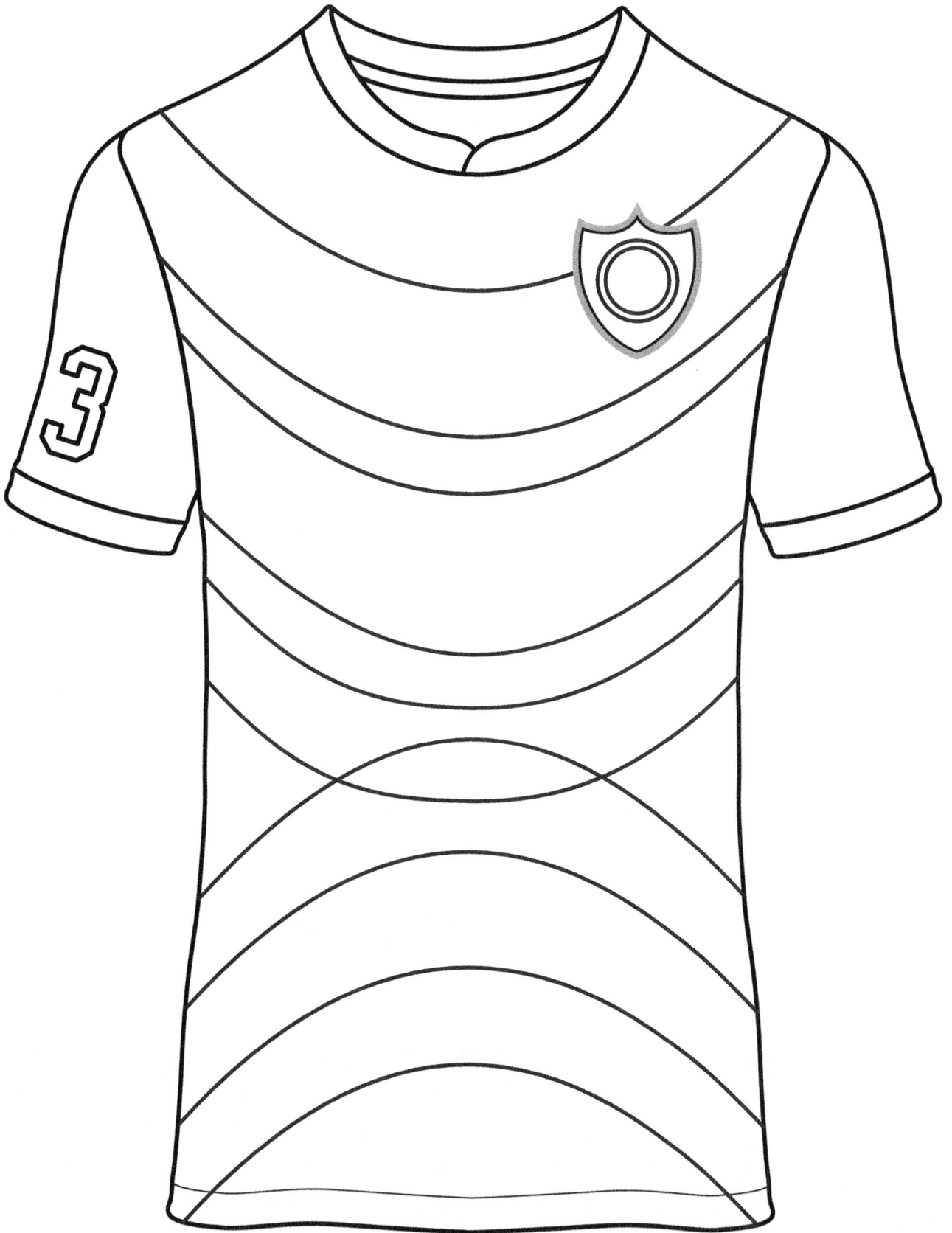

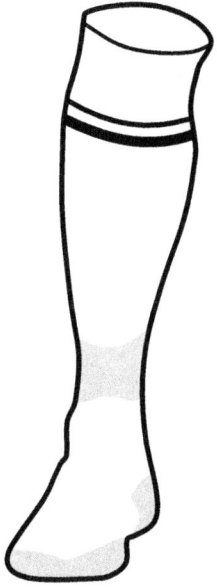

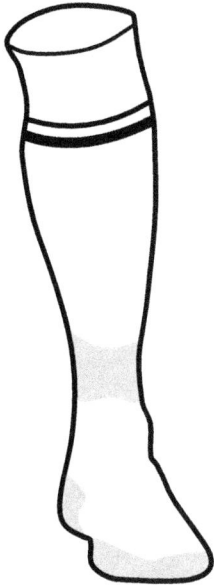

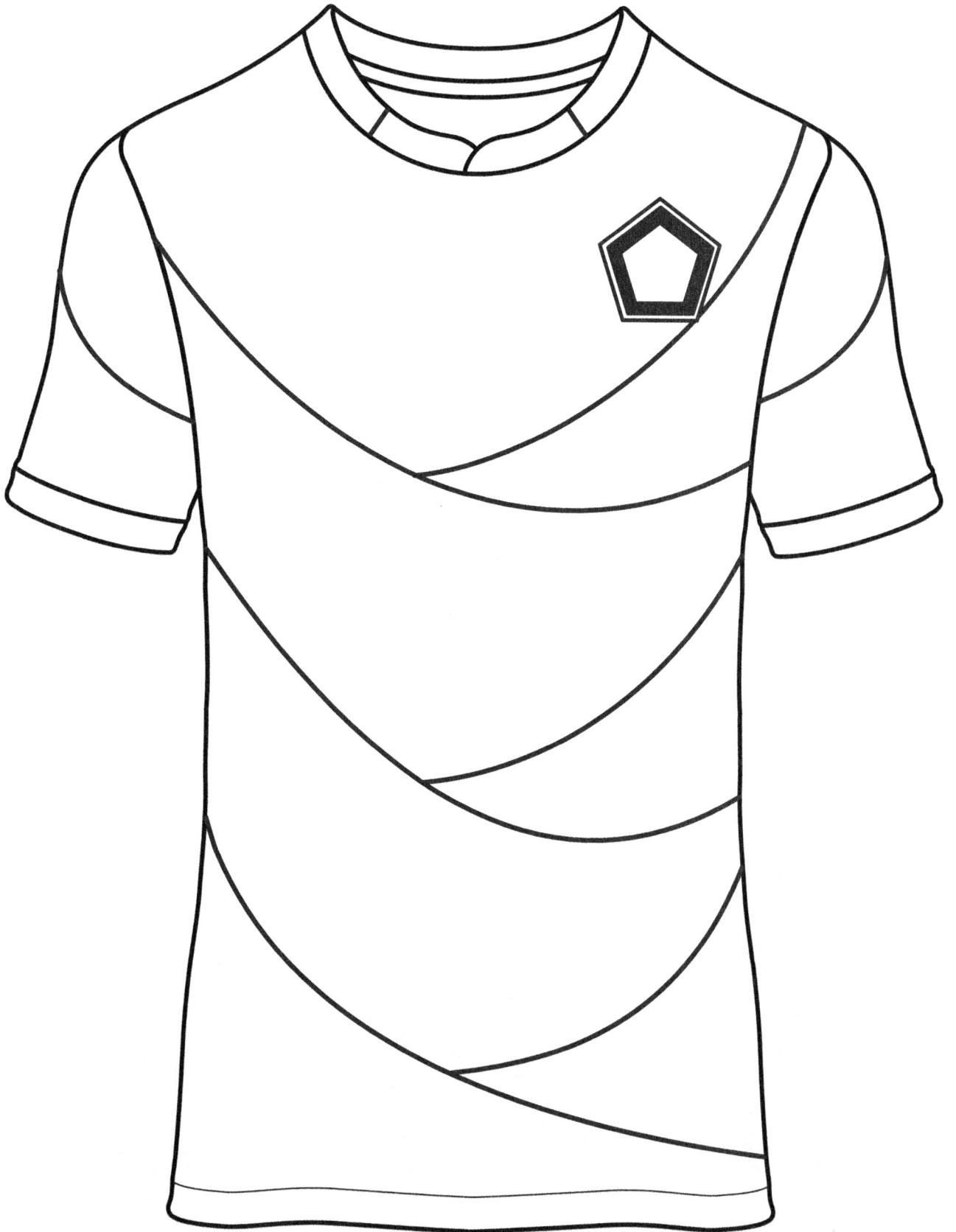

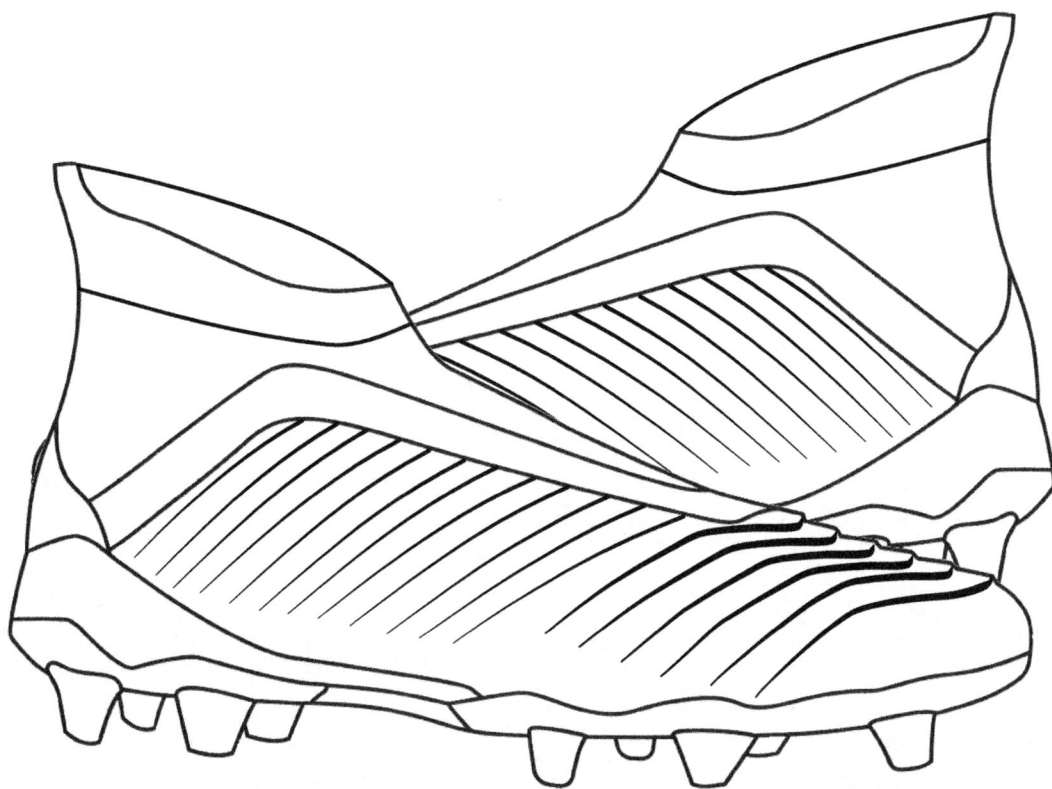

FOOTBALL BOOTS

STAR PLAYER

Printed in Dunstable, United Kingdom